To all my mothers and fathers.
To all my brothers and sisters.
To all my sons and daughters.
You have walked beside me constantly.

So much became possible
when I consciously and decidedly
opened to the love and support available to me
in every form
in every exchange
in every moment.

I look at each of you
and see myself over and under again.
It is everything to feel you with me.

This book is from all of Us.
This book is for all of Us.

Bless,
Meg

Words
Collected
on the
Road to
Silence

MESSAGES TO ME

MARGARET COYLE

Meg's poems dance in my body. A magnitude of remembrance rushes through me as I read the *One Love* that flows through her being and all beings. Meg is a mystic and her being invites my heart to stretch, knowing that all is well and whole. The rhythmic dance of her poetry moves one's breath beyond the constrictions of a small identity. She enters the moment exactly as it is and challenges fear's need to split wholeness and connection. She touches connection with a tender fierceness and extends love's energy and the capacity to open space to dance, to write, to love, welcoming what arrives in the moment. She invites us to know we are all dancing together on love's dance floor.

Ingrid Sato
One who remembers,
inquires and witnesses
her friend, Meg.

Who is the person that has produced this book? We tend to look for letters and papers to certify our knowledge, to certify our authority, to certify even our existence. For me the truest answers are questions. If you get a hold of a really good one, it will move your life for sure. I will leave it to you to follow whatever movement brought this book into your hands and invite you to let it into your heart. It was written from mine, hoping to find yours. If you are looking for credentials, I can say I am foremost, a certified human being, certified by my existence. Of anything I might put behind my name, I am most inclined to put that down as it covers so much that is hard to describe with names or letters after 46 years of living, although dance and poetry help a lot.

I teach and learn with movement relative to the breath. My education has been and continues to be this moment as the breath moves through my body. As every human is doing the same, I have found many others to dance with in the exploration of what it is to be, and what it is to be a human being. The field is rich and the yield from these explorations has been the expansion of my spirit, through faith in something larger than my limited sense of myself.

I am married 25 years to the man I met at 16, and together we have, but do not hold, three astounding daughters. I come from a family of 10, my parents, married 51 years, 7 siblings, and at last count, 29 nephews and nieces. They are an intelligent, compassionate group with a grand sense of humor. My family has been, and continues to be a rich source of support and challenge. I am supremely grateful for the souls included.

May you find loving support for the challenge of allowing your spirit to expand through the witness of my journey as told in these pages. I invite awareness and offer whatever comfort I can as the lies meet the heat of the Truth. These poems arrived in my life when the wounds or the joy got too big for conventional language. They have been my medicine, the thread to weave together again the parts of me torn asunder.

Margaret Coyle
Certified Human Being

MESSAGES TO ME

A feeling
a thought
flies by on a word.
A thought
a circumstance
a sound that you heard.
From Me to Myself
with One Voice given
I call and it is my Holy Self who answers.
With messages to myself I reach for you
and unwavering Love is the sound coming through.
Why would I stay where I don't belong?
With messages to myself
I call myself home.

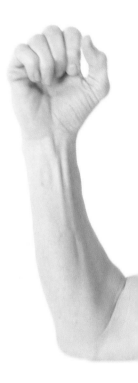

Who Am I ?

Who am I
to think I know the answer
in part or whole.
I feel the warmth
I sense the pulse
I catch fragments but they're hard to hold.
Here we sit
back to back
head to head
face to face
to fix what feels broken
wondering if it's too late.
I'm asking you to see what you're not looking for.
Its a catch-22
maybe catch-44.

I call on your faith to see something hidden
I count on your passion
I hope for your vision.
Hear it call to your worst
that part smothered in fear.
Bravely call on your best
can we love a path clear?

What is our purpose in regard to each other?
What does it mean to be sisters and brothers?
What does it mean to be fathers and mothers?
What does it look like to Love one another?

Who am I?

I am one
who knows this.
My path is a process and I know it to be
the realization and expression of the truth that's in me.
As a daughter, a sister, a mother, a wife
I hold closely the ones supporting this in my life.
In the search for the path that will show you what's true
I support the realization of All that's in you.
I support your expression.
I'll rely on your clues.
To love the path clear
we'll need all the clues.

Who am I?

I'm one
who's speaking for two.
Knowing just because I want it
you do too.
When I find Myself
what can I offer you?
Can we love a path clear?
Do you want my clues?

Bon Voyage

Circling at the dock
I look out at the sea
knowing I will go
knowing I am going now.

Your love is my provision
and reminds me
I'm not alone.

Currents of the past
sweep along my edges.
The tides rip
at my small identity.

I hold you to me
as I go with you.

And so we meet
in the water
that we are.

My God My Friend

You have treated me with remarkable kindness and patience.
My heart is full of countless blessings
and I am thankful for all the precious souls
I have been given to dance with in this life.
In your company
I feel myself in you
and feel you awakening
to your home in me.
You have clearly been One for me
and I One for you.
Your kind and gentle heart has boldly and gently
loved me through the many ways
I have thought to try and cover my beauty.
You have been undaunted
barely blinking at my most masterful efforts
of believing I am less than worthy.

How do I express my gratitude?
Every word falls short
and my earnest desire to know Myself
is the only way I know to honor
the miraculous gift of your love.

I thank you
and with the same words
I thank God
for the truth
as it lives in you
for my eyes for your beauty
as it shows me my own
for your eyes for my beauty
as it returns yours to you.
A circle in this world
filled with the light of Love.

My God
my friend
how perfectly you are woven together in my heart.

STEPPING THROUGH

Locked in convention
mistakes aren't allowed.
Seeking freedom from choices
that would make others proud.
Endless possibilities
just that side of the door.
Stepping through
I drop convention
in a pile on the floor.

MUSIC

We place such emphasis on divide and conquer
denying the music of living.
We must learn again to love each note
and find the faith
to let them find each other in the song
of this moment.

Travelling Home

I can feel it right in front of me
but I don't remember calling it.
What name did I use?

I hardly noticed when everything else disappeared.
And then It was right here
right now.

What are the elements that deliver me to a moment
so clear , so vibrant
where the veil is so thin
that the softest breeze is enough to brush it aside
letting me see the world I have made
undressing
taking off every name?

I look
and see my own names come unbuttoned
and fall to the floor.
Naked with the One
I feel God moving
in me
moving around me
moving through me
loosening the straps of my grip
dropping me further into the pulse
of this single
infinite moment…

And then- - -

The phone rings.
I'm in the dark alley of a bad dream
shivering in the cold

without a dime
or a pocket to hold it in
feeling alone
feeling lost
and feeling panicked.
Sigh…
This can feel tricky.
Beauty is serenading me.
She constantly invites me to return
and…
sometimes I just stop listening.
Swimming in fear can disorient.
I know I only need to hold to her song to carry me
and…
sometimes I let go.
But when I do remember to listen
I hear her sing…
"you can change your mind any time"
every time
I feel the waves roll over my head.
And even in the deepest water
Her vision delivers my feet to the ground.

And so I stand in this day
in my commitment to listen
knowing that when I break down
Beauty's reminders put forgiveness back in my hands.
I use it to call on acceptance
and reopen the roads blocked.
Every time I feel lost
I can lift my eyes
and find again
the house of Light
and move toward home.

I See You Look

You look at me
and see one grain of sand when I am every desert.
You see one drop of water
when I am the oceans.
I see your fears have made your frame too small to hold real vision.
Even the smallest aspect of me
will never be small enough to fit in your pocket.
I cannot keep you safe
as your fear defines safety
that is
anywhere away from the whole.
When I see you
I see All.
Don't ask me to hold you in limit
as I would have to then believe I am less than I Am.
I have moved too far out of that hell
to be fooled back in.
I will no longer fit
and I will no longer try.
Even when the request comes
from your beautiful
frightened
mouth.

FORTY-THREE LITTLE YEARS

Forty-three little drops into an ocean of years that melt into eternity.
I have this day and I'm glad.
I did nothing to earn any of the days that have made up the last 43 years.
It's just luck.
God's gift
Life
right in my hands!

My response is simple gratitude.
I can't see another part for myself.
So I am grateful
and with gratitude
I stand in this day
with a desire
to be more awake
to be more alive
to love
to see this day as it really is
not what I imagine it to be.

With my feet on the earth
I move to the rhythm of life
bubbling up from the center of my being.
What a dance!
What partners to be found!
What a blast!

To this day!

It holds the essence of every day of the last 43 years
and the next 43 years
and more.
It's everything
and it's mine to receive and give
right now!

I humbly honor this gift of Life
with a magnitude of gratitude.

I raise my full heart
to all my brothers and sisters this day
and sincerely sing Cheers
to the sky!

Eyes Of Wonder

Eyes of wonder
carry me into the waters of possibility.
Let me lie across your face
and feel your breath along my spine.

I wonder at Love
and I love to wonder.
What children will be born
of this moment I am meeting?

There is strangeness between us now
just as we are partly strangers to ourselves.
I bow to the mystery
and trust in the unknown
as it calls us forward into discovery.

This face so familiar
but still a surprise
holds the shape of a story yet to be fully told.

Time has not diminished my curiosity.
I am indeed more interested than ever!

ONE QUESTION

The truth lies underground.
Its roots run deep in all directions under this big house.

I remember running to keep up
my pockets heavy with promises.
I was only ever fast enough to catch a glimpse
as you slipped through another door.

There are so many doors in this house.
These days I only know you by your backside.

I can't find the ground to stand eye to eye
as you float through the air.
Will you ever look for me?
Would you recognize me if you did?
It gets harder to imagine.

Meanwhile
I am learning to be quiet.
I am learning to be still.
I am learning to trust the feeling of devastation
as this house falls around my ears.
I am learning to listen for the song in all of it.

My head is full of questions
and the only answer I can hear
is a single question.

How do I choose to live my life?

APPETITE

I will swallow all the pain
all the joy of this world
the whole strange mix.
I will bite
chew
swallow
and digest it all
sending Love into the bloodstream
of the One Body.

Look at the plants that chew the rocks
and release the same minerals into my body
when they break against my teeth.
I too am food for life.
I desire to be broken
to be chewed
to be swallowed and transformed
into the bones
and flesh
and blood of the Truth.

Look at me.
Smell me.
Gaze until your mouth waters.
Let your appetite build
and savor the empty space in your belly.
Move from your hunger.
Come and take a bite.
You are not stealing.
You have been invited to this table.
Fill your plate.
Let me feed your heart with my heart.

TELL ME

What does it feel like to behold me?
And the question to hold in front of every question put to you is this -
From where is the question being asked?

I will tell you from where I am asking.
I am asking from my flesh
from my bones
from my blood
from my breath.
I am asking from the place in me that knows every answer
before a question is spoken.
I am asking for your experience of the One
in this moment
as You see It in Me.

Stay alert.
There is an imposter in this world.
He can show up in any of us at any time.
Keep an eye out for him on the street and in the mirror.
He will ask for the biggest thing from the smallest place.
He is gripped by the insatiable desire for things of the world.
He is alone in his castle
with locks on the doors to hold every thing in
and locks on his heart to keep every one out.
Without a vehicle to experience his fortune
his only response to his desire to seek
is to keep seeking
never having.
He is driven by the masses of life piling up before him
yet he starves with no way to eat.

My door is wide open to a question that is whole.
A whole desire to know me
will carry you right across the threshold
and into my heart.

Help yourself to me
and help myself to you.
Let me in.
I welcome you.
We will have the most glorious time pouring into each other.
With nothing to lose
we can be free to Love.
With everything to Love
We can rest
in peace
Tell me.
What does it feel like to behold me?

SMALL FIRES

There appears to be more than one way to the truth
and so there are for you in the times you believe it to be so.
Believing the Truth to be debatable
allows the delusions of the world you see
to disprove what is real
and supports a world of illusions.
Be still.
Find a place you feel safe
and begin with small fires
burning off
whatever you can let go of.

FLYING/FALLING

Flying across a thousand years
I am riding high above the changing tides
and shifting currents of my mind.
At every point in time
I stand between the stories of my past
and the stories of my future.
Pushing up from the center
toward the light of this day
my desire to move forward on this line stands tall
its face washed in shadow.
A city of sweet ache sprawls out from the center of my chest
shifting like a weather front
as it moves across the geography of my body.
The humidity is rising and the air is thick with anticipation.
The sun is high as I stand in the center of the street
squaring off to step forward and meet Myself.
The arms of desire reach long for my coming.
My ears crane to hear the song of my arrival.
I look out and see my heart moving toward me from every direction.

This moment that has held my imagination captive
moves closer.
Its breath hovers at the back of my neck
poised to caress or bite?
I'm not sure and I stand ready to love either way.
I stand willing to let vision knit it All back together again.

I am a ripe pear about to let go of this branch.
I open my eyes and see myself falling
as certain as I can be
that the earth will catch me
one way or another.

WELCOME

Tell me your secrets.
You're safe.
There is only you
and me
and the moon.

I won't say a word
but I have to tell you
the moon is repeating them to the wind
even as you whisper them so close to my ear.
By now word is travelling across the hills
and into the ear of every strand of golden grass on the rolling hills.

The summer has been long and dry
and there is such thirst for a juicy story.
And so your secrets spread.
It's a wild fire.
The hills are wild with the fire of your story.
The smoke billows up
into the air
and under the wings of every passing flock
who pump your most tender secrets
down on the heads of every creature.

Within no time there is no longer a place
that is not covered with the most intimate news of you!
In that same moment your reason for hiding dissolves.
Look at me now and see your self revealed.
Welcome!
How I have longed for your sweet naked smile.

Two Hearts

Two hearts opened create space
enough to absorb all of time and space.

Carried on the back of one conscious moment
are bits of stories
emotions
and memories
pieces of a dream.

Precious babies are born
of two joined in their attentiveness
to the presence of presence
pouring down on them
filling every space
pushing out what is not–
the hurt feelings
the judgments
the prejudices.

Of course
these beloved children must grow up
and test the lie that they could fail.

If they flap their wings in the wind
they will learn
they can always fly
even if the world tells them otherwise.

WHAT DOES IT FEEL LIKE TO SAY I LOVE YOU?

The question feels like golden space
in a precious heart
opening to be filled
with my truest answer.

It feels like a divine invitation
to step into a holy lake
and I am salt.
I dissolve into the water
and We become
an ocean of Love
giving birth
to diverse
and miraculous things.

I am just starting to answer this question.
It will take a lifetime.
A thousand poems will be born
as each moment steps up
to give their answer
to the question
I am so blessed
to be holding.

SINGLE EYE

Spend time looking from the center
where distinctions are not knives to cut.
Truth sees Truth with a single eye.

Yes!
Stretch
Yes!
Fly
Yes!
Say yes and wonder by.

A kite dipping and lifted
form slipping and shifted
over and under and under and through
all time
spinning
as a child
get dizzy and fall
watch it all
swirl
from my back
in the lap
of the Mother
helplessly
faithful.

I turn my head to the right
and see you
and those crazy eyes full of light.

God I love that!

Life Shared

As I know you in this moment
and as we drop together deeper still into this union
the depth of knowing keeps reaching further and further back
into all the moments of my life
like a vine
patiently
methodically
instilling itself into and around every moment.
There will be no untangling its winding presence.

Meanwhile the moments of my future
are gathered like excited schoolgirls.
They long and wonder with anticipation
which of them will be chosen
to hold your precious company.

Those chosen
move into a category of standing
held in the highest regard by my heart.
Those chosen are transformed.
They are humbled by the immense gift of Love
now written on their bodies.

They will forever live as a reminder
of what is possible.
Their life forever dedicated
to awakening every moment in time
to the broadest possibilities
the fullest expression
of this precious gift

A Life shared.

HOUSE OF GOD

My heart is stretching
expanding to hold all the Love
coming toward me from every direction.
I can't bear to watch even a speck fall unclaimed
so I pick up every one
without judgment
without prejudice
even when it feels my heart is so full it will burst.

I exhale and uncover more space.
With every cycle of breath I am remade
over and over
a hundred times
a million times
for all time.

This Spirit is so great
this Love is so big
I will forever be yielding
to its incessant invitation to expand
and my matching desire
to house God in my very being.

What Is This Moment?

Floating in a pool of time
the shifting currents tickle my ivories.
Harmonies lift off my skin
and rise with the heat of the Light.
I watch the clouds float by.
Moments of time
dance to the rhythm of the blowing breezes
illustrating the story of my life.

What is this moment?

A man
with a boy's heart
and the sun's face
steps forward on the air
his hands filled with flowers.
A bouquet of invitation
to every part of my being
is extended in his arms.

What is this moment?

A girl
with a heart full of pain
a stomach full of pills
a head full of questions
and despite it all
a life full of possibility.

What is this moment?

A baby
with the universe suspended in her smile.
Every planet orbits around me

in her reaching arms
popping my heart
like a party favor.

What is this moment?

Warm ground under my back
holding me like a rose petal in the late summer
fallen from the flower
intoxicated by her own sweet scent.

What is this moment?

Laughter
dropping me off the top of a cliff
rocks passing me down to the bottom
with pillowed hands.

What is this moment?

The ground is torn out from under me.
My heart erupts violently.
The light feels like salt
in an open wound of festering lies.
All of this dances in a huge field
with comfort now rising in equal measure
to the deepest pain I have ever known.

What is this moment?

Ideas of truth
like playground bullies
pushing and shoving
with Grace stepping in to restore peace
again. ☞

And this one?

The blue of the time sky pours into my eyes
filling my body until I know only that
I Am.

This present moment
is the very canvas for all these moments to sing.
My faith conducts a symphony of perfection
as every cell of my body grows quiet
opening further
to the privilege of vibrating
with the sacred sound of the One.

I am disarmed
and remembered
at the same time.

I saw the sun this morning.

After billions of years of waking this world
its passion so fresh
it washed everything down to the beginning.
The heat of its kisses fell everywhere without exclusion.

I saw the sun lay on the river.
There was a wild exchange of heat and light
as children of water and fire were delivered to every direction.

Standing on the bridge
the river's sighs ran up my legs
flooding my being
and swallowing my fences.

I am no virgin no matter how I protest.
I have been opened.
I have been entered.
My denial can no longer hold back
the heat rising in my chest.
It melts my resistance
and falls from my eyes.

Water to Water

This dance runs through my veins.
This dance is my blood.
My protests grow faint
in the roar of the current.
My longing tears at my seams
ripping me
cutting me
bleeding me
freeing me.
Spirit I pray.
Unthaw my frozen feet.
Throw me in this river.
Wash the denial from my heart and mind.
Let me be moved.
Let me return to the water that I am.

The Leaf

It was some spring that a leaf was born into being.
It started small and tender
and grew to be deep, green, and strong.
It nourished the tree it was hanging from
by joyfully doing the work of a leaf.

The leaf danced with the other aspects of the tree
and together they produced colorful flowers, sweet smells
fruit to eat and shade from the heat.
Together they produced inspiration to fill every heart.

The leaf was so happy to feel himself
at the center of such a beautiful dance.
He could see his joy extend everywhere he looked.

Now it was some Fall and the leaf could feel
it was some time for him to leave the branch
that had held him in the rain, and the wind
the branch that had taken the sun from his face
and carried it to the rest of the tree.
The branch he loved.
He could feel it was time and he was not sad.
He knew himself to be a part of the tree
before he was a leaf
and now
as the wind lifted him gently
and carried him down
he was so happy
to kiss the sweet earth
and begin again.

Alive With Love

You want to know how it feels?
I'll tell you.
Everything stops swirling and lands right in front of you.
You are stunned by the vision of It
beside you
inside you.
It is hard to believe It
and effortless to know It.
Whatever conclusions you were drawing a moment before
fly from your mind like an arrow
landing all of time into a single point
expanding your cells
warming your body
charging your heart
and outlining your soul.

Wave after wave of love
and living
and loving
wash over you
turning you around and over in a sea of laughter
and touch
and grace
and generosity
and breath.
They ease you over angles of cheeks
and slide you down necks.
They float you past elbows
and collect you in hip bowls
They crash you against pelvises
and wash you up on the shores of surrender.

And there are these eyes
that travel all the way into your center
and reflect it back to you.

There is a song in your ear that sings all of this to you
and you can hear it even from the page.
Beauty rises to engulf you and every other
as your smiles float to the top
with a song of gratitude to God
for the blessing it is to know
that you are alive with Love.

What is the sound of my calling?
I listen and I hear.
This day
what a witness you are!
I see you
me.
I hear you
me.
I feel my inquiries weaving
you
me
We.
I am alive and singing
fluidly
powerfully
gracefully.
I feel my balance.
Driving out of range I see it arching over me
broad as the sky over my head
and as specific as the grain of sand under my foot.
All of this
dancing in my body
animating these arms
directing these legs
giving shape to this intention
in this moment
on this spot.

I say Yes!

Someone is cooking something really delicious
and the wind is blowing it my way.

When fear pollutes your needs
there is no road for me to arrive in your experience.
When fear creeps in anywhere
it creeps in everywhere.
Attempting to live through the impossibly small opening of your fears
will distort and mangle every call for Love
as you speak it and as you listen for it.
Warped and mangled by your fears
you will become a walking wreck.
Every word you speak will be hedged with sadness
naming you sad
and calling sadness to you.
Every action you make will be saturated with desperation
marking you desperate
and coloring your days with darkness.

When you are sad enough
when you are desperate enough
when you are tired enough of being sick and tired
you will finally become brave enough
to give yourself over completely
and so find the way.

And it will cost you everything you think you are.

When you have given everything over to your desires
the deepest
the truest
the most mysterious and powerful desires of your heart
when you have fed everything you think you have
everything you think you are
everything you come across in this world
to this ravenous heart
including your mind

While fear demands *when* and *where*
the truth knows only now
this moment
this breath.

The Truth invites me to be still and rest.
The Truth invites me to be still and be healed.
While fear would have me dig in search of what was lost
consumed with regret and resentment
the Truth knows only that I Am
and nothing else.

In the garden
my eyes fill with color
and I see I Am.

In the quiet
my ears fill with song
and I hear I Am.
With this breath
my nose fills with sweet scents
and I am reminded
that I Am.

My skin is graced with the warmth of the Son
as I look in
and breathe in
the comfort of remembering
I Am
Now.
Holding this certainty in my body
displaces every dis-ease
and leaves me at ease.

As I practice forgiveness
my heart bends the bars of my rib cage with bare hands

releasing me from my prison
Outside the bars
I can see the space
for a whole poem of loving
for the whole joy of living
for the full fire of knowing
the Truth of Love needs nothing
and it is everything.

I am grateful
for the space to practice
to be reminded
and to remember.

GRACE

It is a beautiful sparkling morning.
Love is what I am
and Love is what I am in.
This morning
I know this more than anything else.
Less real this morning
is a life out of Love.
And so I feel what this feels like
and continue over and over
under and over again
to understand
to stand under
to understand
what is true
what is true.
I let go of narrow eyes
grow new ones
let go of those
let go of my tongue
grow it back
and let go of that one.
I let go of arms and legs
and I am re-membered
again and again
as my body
my being
my body
my being
are transformed
and reformed
and transformed.
I am here
in the world I see
moving through ☞

breathing the air and feeling my heart.
I know you feel me.
I feel you here as well.
It is no small measure of grace
to know that we are not apart.

I AM THAT

Seeking the deepest
widest
most intimate
relationship with God
I move into
around
and through my theologies
my ideas of God.
I move into
around
and through
my emotions
my feelings about God.
I move into
around
and through
my intellect
further
deeper
wider
in
and around
and through
until I land
where

I Am.

Standing naked with the One
there is not the thinnest shred of anything
between me and God.
I Am That.

God is
my thoughts
God is
my feelings
God is
my mind
God is
my laughter
my tears
my dance
my song
my joy
my sorrow.
God is not an idea.
God is.

I am That.

A POEM

I want to carry a long and flowing poem that rings with the delight and ease, the humor and intimacy, the beauty and simplicity of sharing this Love. Like Mary, I am afraid, and willing at the same time, aware of all it will bring down on my head in this world of bad dreams. At the same time, I know I cannot say no to it and be happy.

I want to carry this precious poem to term and deliver it with all the pain and blood and labor of birth. I want to hold it in my arms, feed it at my breast and care for it as it grows, and then send it forward into the world with my blessing, to sing of the times we have known of Love in this world, to sing of the times we are knowing right now, and the times we will know, until time is no more.

It will be an epic poem, falling from the Mind of God to my mind, through my heart, out every cell of my body, and into the expectant ears and eyes of every other with the willingness to see and the desire to hear. It will light on their minds, reaching down to the center of their hearts, and will ring in them the very same and perfect tone of gratitude for the awareness of God's gift of each other, to each other, through each other.

I call on the memory of my innocence and the innocence of all my brothers and sisters, so we can allow all that can come through us to continue, in the simplest and most glorious ways. I will humbly watch each one exposed to this poem unfold like a flower in the sun, as God delivers the Light through me. I am a vehicle, and this is my purpose. It answers my most fervent desire in this life, to remember, and wakefully contribute to Love, the dance of it, the knowing of it, and nothing else. I want to ride believing all the way down to knowing, and in knowing, become single minded, and infinitely powerful in the expression of Love in this world.

As God calls each of us to write, and sing, and dance, and paint, and breathe our poems, I pray to consciously and enthusiastically receive all the light coming through my brothers and sisters. I pray to receive All of God through them and joyfully allow their light to reflect off all of my facets as I move in this world.

I wish to Love every one I see or even think of, so fully, so completely, that everywhere they go, they will spill over and soak everyone they meet with the same Love.

I am grateful for every other who is practising with me today, and all the days to come. I humbly and gently love my practice and theirs, just exactly as it's showing up this very moment. It's all so precious, the contact the laughter, the tears, the dialogue, the deepening trust and the blossoming friendship with the truth. The walk is simple, and sweet and big. It is so full, so rich. My heart is open and continues to expand by the Spirit.

I have planted a thousand kisses on the heart of every being through my prayers and words and actions. I imagine each of these kisses taking root in their bodies, making of them walking gardens, marking their beings with Love. I will continue to water carefully and prune when necessary, under the direction of the wisdom within me.

I am committed to setting hearts on fire!

Yes

I have been working to hold you since the day I thought I saw you. I have worked and grabbed but never felt satisfied. I gripped and blamed and when I could not feel you, I thought the problem must be that you were not the right size, that you were not the right shape. So I tried to rename you so you could fit into my hands and we could be together. I named and renamed until I saw it was You that I desired. It was You, not my names of you. I redirected my work and pushed the knot to the other end. I tried to change the shape of my hands so that I could hold you and we could be together. I stretched my hands, I trimmed them, I measured, and planned, and I tried so hard, until I saw that without Me, I had nothing to hold You with.

Now I am looking for every effort and releasing it. I am slipping forgiveness into the dark and rusted keyhole of every story I have written to reconcile what can never be reconciled–the idea of you or me. With forgiveness, the doors are opening. With forgiveness, the walls of every plan and every posture are cracking and crumbling. Forgiveness is setting us free, forgiveness is uncovering the Truth that was, the Truth that is, the Truth that ever will be.

Now, I am asking to see, and I am quietly, faithfully, waiting to be shown. And this is what I see. There was only ever a divine invitation to be with You. Right now there is a divine invitation to be with You being whispered into my ear with the voice of innocence. This invitation asks only for me to say yes.

I am smiling. Yes falls from my eyes, clearing every log. Yes lifts from my skin, cooling every fear. Yes fills my lungs, and Yes sings from my body with every exhale taking my doubts with it. I say yes, and dance yes, and cry yes, yes, yes from every part of Myself, to every part of Myself. I am inviting every other to join Me and find this way Home by marking the path with my joy and gratitude.

Blessed are the eyes to see the invitation.

Blessed is the wisdom in me that answers Yes!

What are these trees springing up? What is this fruit? The shape is strange but the taste is so familiar. Our tongues rush forward to offer themselves to the story being written. A sweet reunion! Of course we know this taste.

It's the perfect Love that we are!

Powerful Medicine

Another moment, another breath in, another breath out, another expression of gratitude for the One Love moving all of life.

You move in and through me easily, outlining the depth and breadth of my heart's opening. You have been an ingredient, stirred into my days, and now after such a time, you have clearly influenced the very flavor of my being. I am more conscious of how delicious I am, you are, We are, God is, life is! I am, full of wonder, and it's wonderful to dance these days in your company.

Beautiful reminders have awakened all the colors of Love, and they are stretching across the horizons of my awareness. It's a joy to be connected, to know it, to feel and smell the truth of It, in silence, and in the sharing of common activities.

The senses of my soul are waking as I feel the collective movement of our minds, beyond our bodies. I have no words to name it exactly, and I am complete in my knowing that Love is real.

When you see me, I am touched, and so I find myself again through your faithful eyes. To hear myself singing in the eyes and ears and mind of another locates me. It's powerful medicine.

THE RAIN

I see the rain come and watch as things grow in response to it, or float, or dissolve. I can see myself, and feel my capacity to do any, and all of these things. It occurs to me how lovely it is to have another to float on, to have others to grow with. It's lovely to bask in the light of a smile and hum along with the song of a soul as it comes to me. It's lovely to dissolve into another as I try on new rhythms, and in meeting those rhythms, find yet another part of myself.

I find the We of you and me.

I know all the elements of circumstance will continuously shape and shift, and so will the shape of our We. All I need is to feel what is, and celebrate it. I am celebrating. It's precious to share this Love, this way, this day.

I am holding you close. I am taking you with me everywhere and you are good company. You are no burden. I welcome you home, in my heart, without limit or condition. I remind you of the welcome that is just for you, the calling of your name specifically and endlessly as if the world could not go on without you, which it cannot. It hungers for you to fall in. This hunger has taken hold of my heart, and my heart sings over and over, your precious name.

I am humbled to be made into an invitation for you to show yourself in this world. I am humbled to feel God write His love for you all over me, and I am humbled by the divine that is in you as It rings the same in me.

It's all so...so... Oh my, it is so.

Sighs lift from my body, a mist rising from the love cascading from my heart. Blessings fall from me, into you, where they fit perfectly.

There is Love.

It's the ground under our feet.

It's the air in our lungs.

It's the fire in our hearts.

It's the vast water of our minds.

It fills us.

It's who we are.

Filling and falling in infinite ways, we learn to trust every form, our laughter and our tears. We are moved gracefully by our dance of acceptance.

Holy Spirit, release us from every idea we hold, that holds us away from each other.

Empty our minds of every effort that binds and weakens us.

Untie every knot, allowing peace to carry us out, and into everything.

Wash us clean of every fear and free us to move, free us to speak, only the light of Love in every moment, to every other. Help us to maintain the balance between what you have written on our hearts and our actions.

We trust the wisdom in us to find the shapes and words for the healing Love that is moving in each of us.

We trust that these shapes and words will fit perfectly in the eyes and ears of everyone whom is brought into our company because we intend it to be so. And, we are grateful to know it is so. And so It Is.

As I grow, I am constantly moving, shaping, and sounding, to meet the light of Love. When I move according to my true desire, there is space, and creation happens in miraculous ways. Experiencing the miracle of Love, awakens my consciousness, and I feel God moving me. When I question my most honest desires, my movement is impossibly small, and my experience of God becomes frail. Away from the light I feel confused. In the dark I feel alone. Without a song I feel sad.

Acknowledging, allowing, and loving my rhythms, deepens my connection to them. It's through the action of trusting and moving from my real Will, that I come to know my connection to the larger rhythms that hold the entire universe and every being, in perfect balance. It's through my faith I find the only thing I want, peace of mind.

The internal and external meet in my body. Away from that center, I'm homesick. I'm always searching, not knowing why, or for what exactly. And...my hearts knows perfectly. So I search, knowing and not knowing at the same time. It's a mysterious act of balancing the twos, the twos that constantly reach for each other to join. My true longing is forever pointing me toward the unknown, and it's in trusting that direction that I find a deep remembrance.

When I lose my way, I inch my way back to the center, however I can, and find again my balance, my peace waiting there for my return. Breathing in I look to the center of my being, the part unseen. Breathing out, I extend that center to the world. I watch the breath as it weaves, in and out, over and under, the beginning and the end, weaving it all, into this extraordinary, tapestry of living.

I am laying under the moon, under stars and storms, and every kind of sky, speaking, singing, and whispering poems into your ear, into the ear of every cell of your body, all day, and all night. Your listening is so active it primes me. Like a siphon, your listening draws the poetry from my heart. I feel it flow, from me into you, until there is no distinction left between speaking and listening. It's all the same.

The exhaust of all of this is a deep sigh, the breath of satisfaction. It resounds from the center of my being, the place where we meet, the place where every difference falls away, the place where we take every thing off and feel the naked truth, together.

I am listening to the pieces of your story. I am humming to the big song under your little words. I am watching, and I am curious about how the song rings in you. I wonder... what does it shake loose, what feels hard, and what feels simple about it? I wonder what I might lend to it all, and I feel my desire to know you, my desire to hear you and be near you, my willingness to listen, is everything. And all I want is everything.

I want to mix my paints with those God sends to me, in wild and faithful ways. I want to lend my mind and heart, my arms and legs to God inspired experiments in Love. I recognize that not everyone runs their Love lab like me. Some are distinctly different from mine in appearance, yet I know that all experiments in Love are matched in their intention. They are the same in essence, even if they are different in their manifestation.

We are all on our way Home. The cause is the truth we meet around, and the effect is particular to the varied expressions of God in the form of each of us. And so the question I am holding is what do I need in this moment relative to my purpose? The answer I hear return to me is faith. All I need is faith, trust in what I truly want. I truly want to remember. I truly want to awaken.

There is still thinking in me that urges predictions and projections around my thoughts and feelings in this moment. But even the best plans, the most intricate strategies outside of faith always tip over don't they? Everything out of order will wobble, and so everything lacking the balance of faithful intention is exposed if I am honestly looking.

The Truth welcomes any kind of experiment, as it invulnerable. The lies fear every real experiment, as they are completely vulnerable. I am seeking the Truth. I am willing to test my mind. And when I fall, I know I will land on my faith. Again and again, I arrive home to my faith, and through faith, I see it's enough.

I let the story of my life be built according to the infinitely intelligent, loving flow of Life, moving through me as my breath. This flow is the ultimate reality, regardless of what I decide about it. Thankfully my deceptions cannot alter the Truth. It remains perfectly intact,

unharmed, and undiminished in any way.

I am, we all are, subject to the Truth, and I trust It, except when I don't, but those places get exposed quickly with the experience of anxiety. Regardless of circumstance, when I stand in faith, I am peaceful.

Can you hear the cry of my longing for God? Can you feel me reaching to touch my home in you? If you are yourself identified with the Truth, you will hear the cry for what it is. You will understand when my arms reach for you over and over, running over the shape of you, the stories of you, I am moving from my deepest longing to find, and hold Myself in every curve of your being.

I deeply appreciate when another is willing to exercise their desire to hold the larger context of living, while getting very specific with me.

The broadest, most inclusive statement I can make is this-

God is.

I am

and so It is.

Beginner, from the perspective of the intellect, is a job full of effort. There are theories and techniques to collect, places to get to, and deadlines to meet.

As the collections amass, the mind becomes crowded. The intellect alone is not built to hold the infinite, ever expanding Truth of all that we are. And the gathering is just one part of a larger process.

In time, the collections of theories and techniques gathered by the intellect are exposed to experience. Through faith, they find relationship to the whole of living and become aspects of the unified story. It's here the job of surviving, where you or another could succeed or fail, win or lose, becomes the dance of living, where you accept the process as it presents itself in this moment, and simply enjoy it.

This transformation is a miracle and not of our direct doing.

It's a gift.

You will recognize it when anxiety becomes ease, when the complex becomes simple, when the confusing becomes direct, when the vague becomes powerfully clear. When you extend from this place you see all things are steered from the quality of your consciousness.

Surrender your mind, and all that it has collected, to your heart. Drop it all the way down into the center of your being, like a rudder into the hull. The intellect can never make its contribution to the direction of your life sitting up on deck. Faith will help you drop your rudder down, and join once more your intellect with the Wisdom of your being. With your life intact, feel faith steer you through every kind of weather. Feel the Spirit fill your sails. When you release your trying, you will find yourself delivered to your knowing. This is solid ground indeed.

I Am Rich

I am rich. There is so much love in my heart. I have love to burn, love to freeze, love to scatter on the winds, landing on the heads and in the hearts of every other. I let it All pour out from me and find everything and everyone, like the rain, falling indiscriminately. Only the action of clutching and holding back can diminish my fortune, while extending it increases it in every imaginable form.

Today I give Love every way I can imagine, while holding a prayer to continue receiving inspiration to know that this is All I need, that this is All I want. This moment, I give all the ways I can, in every place I am, to all people, in all times, to the end of time. I step out of the clothing of my prejudice, and in my nakedness I see I am plainly kind and simply gentle.

Every moment is miraculously bursting with opportunity to exchange this gift of life. It's happening with intimacy and intricacy beyond my capacity to direct or understand. I let go, and fall all the way into the flow of Love in action. Love moves my arms, Love chooses my steps, Love directs my words and my thoughts. I am, Love in action. I am, and I am grateful for the Love that moves me, and moves through me, connecting me to every other. I am grateful for the eyes to see and the mind to know this is so.

I Choose What This Day Chooses For Me

I am grateful for all that I am, the joy and the sorrow of me. There cannot be one without the other. They are unto each other as we are All unto each other. I celebrate every aspect of the One Body, and welcome the arrival of awareness like a long lost relative.

I choose this day and what it chooses for me. I am in the heart and body of God and I add my willing acceptance of all that presents itself according to the infinite loving wisdom that is my mother and my father. In this day, I hold and join into One, my memory of the past, and my longing for the future, in the center of my heart. I love myself in every other. I love our present capacity to live honestly, and our trust in the constant expansion of Life. My single prayer is not a request, but a statement of inclusion, naming my place at the center of All of It. This naming marks the ground for me to stand in this world.

I dedicate myself to living as authentically and intentionally as I am able in this moment. I give myself to the honoring of all life, through my deeds and my actions, and my faithful witness. I invite every other to dance with me, to every rhythm, the softest breeze, and the fiercest hurricane. I am, and I am all of It.

It's my purpose to share myself. My only fulfilment in being is this exchange, as the atonement calls for it.

I feel myself, and become real in this world through the extension of my heart's desire-to love.

I intend to share the gifts of love, joy, and peace with everyone.

And so I do, in smiles and hugs and loving thoughts, humor and every manner of gladness. I extend and lift the world up, transforming the bad dream into the promise of heaven on earth.

I give, and open my arms and heart so that others may feel themselves when I receive them fully. Through them I am found.

LISTENING

Our questions are answered in direct proportion to our willingness to listen. We think we are waiting for the Truth to find us when really the Truth is waiting to be revealed through the act of our listening. Dressed in nothing but our intention to be shown, we let our listening carry us all the way in. Using forgiveness to cut it loose, we release the past and give time over to perfect order. Releasing ourselves from our efforts we relax and so rest in this practice of listening and looking. We welcome the voice of Truth, the sight of Truth, the smell and taste of Truth, the comfort of Truth. Resting, we let ourselves be filled.

There is an infinite flow of blessings pouring down, and around us, calling only for our gratitude, not as payment, but as the natural response to this gift of life.

It's a blessed practice to cultivate the awareness of our part in this dance. As we allow ourselves to be moved, we're carried through the dream of illusion into the light, where joy is clearly and fully present. Whatever sickness is in us, the remedy is there also. Everything is inside of us right now.

By the light of truth, I see my real Will. It's the Will I share with God, and it's perfect. I put down every argument today, and move into full agreement. I know my intention is all the Spirit requires to lift me out of confusion, and tune my focus to real vision. As I move, I know I go with God. Even when I forget, I know God holds me closely. My prayer to know is answered right now, even when I fail to listen. This is my confidence. This is my ground.

I thank God for everything, in every form, kisses and crashes, wonder and worry, friends and foes, hurt and healing. It's all joined in the name of Love. It's my Will to return completely to this knowing, by forgiving everything. I see It's all unfolding miraculously before me, after me, and through me. My only true response is gratitude, and so I thank God for It All.

God, this day we trust You are real, and governing in the broadest sense, every thing that happens in this world. This morning we move forward to cast our vote according to our will. We acknowledge that in the purest sense our real Will is shared with you. And so we seek this day, to cast our vote from the center of our being, and not from the clouded confused place of fear that tells us we are separate. We remember that the United States, and the process of these elections, are all ultimately directed according to the Laws of Love. Help us remember that distinctions in the manifestation of the One Love, in all the colors, rhythms and textures of this country and this human race, are not divisions, but aspects of You.

We seem to choose between, yet every choice is from the whole and returns to the same. We remember that when we are afraid, we feel these distinctions as attack. When we do, we ask for help in returning to the broadest sense of Ourselves.

Help us forgive every idea that we are separate and see that we are One. Open our hearts so that we can be filled with the knowledge of your Spirit pouring down on us, bubbling up through us, and permeating every aspect of our lives. Help us remember that we only need to remember who we are. Help us to remember that there is no conflict.

This day we step back, and with the eyes of Christ, we see the Whole of Us, perfectly united on the canvas of the One Mind, and we are grateful. We are grateful for this day and all that it provides us. Lead us not into the temptation that we must attack one another, and deliver us from the nightmare that we are apart. Let our clearest knowing of You and our real Will, guide our hands as we vote today at the polls, and every day as we bring our minds completely under your direct guidance. Help us remember that every thought we think is a vote in creating the world we see.

Today we are determined to see differently and so we shall. As we ask Truth of Truth we will receive it. We seek to hold the larger perspective of what is true about this day, this moment, and make the best choices from our collected intention, which is ultimately to know You more clearly. Bless us, and let your blessings be known to each of us, through each other.

SALVATION

Salvation is a statement of my true identity. Miracles are inherent in the truth of what I am, and so I expect them. I ask no more than what is true. God is, and I am of God. I share All with All. All is whole and holy. I am under God's law not the law of this world. Salvation is deliverance from every illusion, and it's God's Will, therefore it is also mine.

I am the means for Salvation. I become an active part by recognizing this and claiming it without doubt or hesitancy. I release every false claim on my identity, and find myself in God. I am entitled to miracles. They are a natural occurrence because of who I am, because of what I am. Today I do not trade miracles for grievances. I only want, and I want only what belongs to me according to the Truth. I relinquish everything else. Thy will be done!

BLESSINGS MY FRIEND

I am meeting this day, with determination to move through the clouds, into the perfect light at the center of my being. I am determined to shine it out to every place and person under the influence of the delusion that there is darkness. I am taking you with me, you are light and easy to hold and that's not because of anything you did or didn't do, it's the truth of you. I love you my precious friend, lover, brother, sister, father, mother. Let your heart be peaceful. Let it welcome every turn, holding to your knowing that you are, One with God, because it's so. Blessings on you this day, and all days, until days are no more.

WAKING

I went to bed and the world looked one way. I woke and it looked completely different. Waking to God is new sight. Waking in God removes the illusions and exposes radiance. As I look up at the gray sky, I can believe that there is no sun, and, at the same time I know it's shining still. I have flown up above the clouds on days that appear gray and I have seen it is so. Remembering this, I look again. When I remember the Promise, what God has given me, compared to what I think I have, I am delivered in an instant, from a land of dread, to a wonderland. It's magical and musical and full of light. All the noise is blanketed. I rest in the quiet and warmth of this moment, lightly humming praises to God…la la la la la mmm mmm mmm…

VISION

I look at this day. First I see what I am looking through, my ideas and prejudices about what I need, where I need them, and when. I fix my eyes on what I think I see and keep looking, letting my intention burn through the layers. I know I have arrived at vision when whatever is in front of my eyes inspires absolute gratitude.

Vision inspires a song of thanks and praise for this moment. It inspires awareness for infinite possibilities. It inspires enthusiasm for loving fully. It inspires a deep appreciation for the perfect formulation of each circumstance just as it is presenting itself.

I feel and see God's hand in every detail, knowing that even when I have the thought that I am not where I intended to go, I know I am forever and always, exactly where I need to Be. I pray to remember this more than I forget it, and to live this knowing, consciously and passionately in alignment with my real Will, the Will of God. So Be It.

The Breath Of Satisfaction

Exhaling fully, I let go of every idea, every effort, knowing that truth does not need me to do anything to be true. Through faith I tune to what is so. When I am aligned, awake, to who I am, to my purpose, every question is answered. In the light of this space I remember that there are no questions unresolved. All is answered because there is no separation. All is one, and all is well, right now.

Without a sense of separation, there is no conflict, no debate about right or wrong, there is only what is. With every conflict resolved there is only one response to life-gratitude, for the air, for the water, for the fire of living. There is exhilaration and inspiration in the sun rising, in the stars at night, in the architecture of a flower, in the expressions crossing a face, in the sensations running through my body. Every aspect of life is a reward and a gift. Nature bears witness to the magnitude of God, and the continual creative force that is moving All of It.

Today as I step from my bed and feel the pull of gravity, I lift my voice in thanks and praise, adding it to the whole of nature's song. It's a unanimous and harmonious chorus of praise and glory to God. All Thanks be to God. All thanks be. Thanks be to God.

Folded Paper

The Holy Spirit unfolds the paper with the truth written on it. Unfolded I can read it clearly. What appeared divided, I see now is whole.

There is not lover and loved at the source, but simply Love, whose aspects rise in my ear like the varied notes of a single song. I feel my sorrows crumble and wash away in the melody laid out before my eyes, releasing me. It feels delicious to move across the full page of this moment into the fullest expression of living.

Stretching

Facing our fears and courageously questioning them is the exercise that will bring us to our real strength in God. Every fear faced, every lie questioned, will expose the reality of Love.

We must look where our fears tell us we must not. We must do what our fears tell us we cannot. While our fears will persuade us to expect failure, our faith will show us we cannot fail.

Through the Holy Spirit we expect life, and love, and blessings, and more life, and love and blessings, and healing, and more.

We lean expectantly into life, and let the darkness of our fears be cast out by the light. This exercising is not without sensation and we welcome the stretching necessary for us to come to hold the infinite space of the Truth.

Take Comfort

Beautiful being, precious child of Light, you don't need words to deliver your beauty. My eyes to see, carry it to me with every breath. Lovely children are born of our meeting, smiles, and tears and exquisite sighs. The vision of you provides me all of this, expanding my ideas of living, coloring everything and everyone I see with the full spectrum of light.

Rest your mind in this knowing and let your body follow. Your faith in God's Wisdom will untie every knot. And so let it all fall from your hands, and wash down the stream. All will find its place in time as you let it. All will blend into the One Holy Instant. Release your plans and receive peace of mind. Withdraw from organizing, and let the Love in you flow out as It Will…Quiet now…The Silence is holding you. The Silence holds all of Us. Remember and Rest precious one.

Single Eye

When my eye is single, I am aware of Wonder. From this single point of reference my life is fully balanced. All the elements, the dancing the singing, the laughing the crying, the wondering and the learning, the work and play are all the same and different, moving out from God and returning to the same, seamlessly, joyfully, easily.

I allow all the elements of my day to be outlined in their distinctness but not separated by judgment. The Love, the light of Christ is the single thread that holds all the pearls of my life, all the precious pearls of every human experience together on One perfect strand of creation.

I acknowledge the power of creation, and that I am empowered by the very power that created me. I recognize that every thought that moves in me is creating by the same power. I desire to understand this more fully and allow my mind to be directed according to the Truth.

Holy Spirit, teach me, re-mind me so that I am a part of your blessing and healing in this world. I am simply Grateful, It has All been given. I joyfully offer my thanks and Praise.

Peace Of Mind

We are never specifically aware of the very best that we lend to each other. And it's enough to know that we are a blessing in this world, simply because we intend to be one.

It's my intention to be shown that is the catalyst for my learning and growing. The operative is my willingness to be shown again and again, my mistaken thinking, as my mind is restored. The process is a continual combing, until every resentment is removed, restoring me to the Truth, restoring me to the only thing I want or need, peace of mind.

A Day Of Glory

This day I desire to understand the Truth, to stand under the truth a little bit more. I know I need help to make the Truth meaningful because of all the thoughts I have become accustomed to. I spend my faith now on the vision of Christ, and open to receive something new, knowing that if I catch even a tiny glimpse of the release that is possible, then this is a day of glory for me and every other. I let the noise of the world, the noise of my thoughts fall into the quiet, and I find rest and comfort in the place where every falsehood is laid down.

With this life, with this day, with this breath moving in my body, I express my most complete willingness to be shown what is real, and my willingness to let go of what I have thought to hold instead.

When I am tempted and feel frustrated, I will remind myself of my goal-to remember and understand that All I give, I give to myself.

The Invitation

The invitation has been issued to each of us to cross the line we have drawn in our lives between what we think we know, and move at last, into the larger wisdom that is always calling us.

Loosening our grip on our ideas of what will serve us, of what we think will save us, opens us to the guidance that will lead us into the places held apart by our fears. We move into these places seeking new perspectives, and expose the counterfeit coins we have spent so much energy guarding. With faith and intention, we enter the moving water of our own evolution, the very breath moving in our bodies. We let it carry us out into the deep water of infinite possibilities, where we find our truth our peace, our home, all waiting for us.

Failure

Failure is a reality for me only when I seek goals that cannot be attained. Failure is real to me when I look for the eternal promise in my mistaken illusions. Even when I am under the influence of my misperceptions, there is still in me the memory of another idea. I may lose sight of the Truth, but I have not forgotten It. It is with me always, and holds everything I want. There is no place my missteps can take me that is away from the sound of the Truth calling me back. There is no combination of missteps or mistaken thinking that can cause me to be separate from God. I cast every thought into the fire of forgiveness for purification. When my thinking is burned clean, heaven will be revealed. And the last thought to be burned is the idea of time. Heaven is here right now. I will not delay it by denying its existence, but turn my denial on the lies I have thought to hold instead. Here is where every contradiction will fall away. Here is where the light of Love will fill every space and time.

There is no failure when I seek the Truth. My single eye provides it for me. There is no failure for the One seeking what is real.

Mining

The truth has been placed within my being, waiting to be mined.

Forgiveness cuts through the rocks of resentment that have dulled my capacity to move. Forgiveness clears the way as I travel toward the sound of the Truth calling my name. A symphony of breath and silence directs my journey inward. I trust the space that Truth makes in my life. It clears away the past, and restores me. Restored, I see I am the field where possibilities live and move.

There is the lesson, there is the class, and there is the practice.

There is thought, there is action, and there is form.

The lesson invites a new awareness for the members of the class, for the arms and legs of the One Body. The practice is the combing of this awareness into your mind until the blossoms of a new perspective open, moving the old patterns and ideas of the mind to fall away.

Bring light into the dark, and the darkness dissolves. There is no need to swing a stick. There is no war. There is nothing to win because nothing real can be lost. There is no place to get to, and so you cannot be early or late. Open your Mind, and let the light in. In the light you will see what is real, and your choices will be clear, and simple, and full of ease.

With complete expectancy, invite the light in response to every form of disease. Let the light in, and release yourself to the practice of allowing your movement to become more conscious, more fluid, more seamless, more vital.

Let go, and your mind will turn and return. Like every river running to the ocean, it will mark a path to the source. And as no river is refused, you cannot fail to find your way home.

There is strain in reaching across the ideas of separation. There is effort to bridge every perceived gap. Flood these gaps with forgiveness and see them disappear. Look again and see yourself whole. Every place of tension, every place where movement is burdened, is calling for the same thing. Let the breath carry the miracle of forgiveness into every gap, and let yourself move across, and into the freedom that has been given to you already.

Don't tie your wings when you step out from your past, or you will just move from one prison to another. Let yourself move, how you can, how you are, right now. Love yourself how you can. Love yourself how you are, right now. Spend your attention on the laws of how and what, of cause and effect. You will be shown everything, if you choose to look.

There is thought, there is action and there is form. There is not one without the other and it is all held in perfect order. Loosen your grip on your beliefs and stand firm in the single intention to be shown what is real instead. Empty your hands so they may be filled. Remember that nothing real is ever lost when your fears tell you to clutch or defend.

Refuse to rush, and breathe. Refuse to panic, and breathe. Allow yourself to listen, and breathe. Allow yourself to wait for the voice of God to fill every question in your mind with the breath, and rest.

Tending The Garden

And so I tend to my garden, the plot of mind that has been given me to live in, the plot of mind that provides for my only need, to express the One Love.

Every thought is a seed that will grow in the soil of my life and bear fruit. I only need awareness with which to carefully study the laws of cause and effect. And so I learn which seeds will grow to become weeds, and which ones flowers. I dismiss any thought that I do not share with God before it takes root. I pull my attention from thoughts I recognize to be fearful. I turn away from delusions and let them whither when I find the fruit they bear to be foul to my heart's tongue.

If I look, I will see, and when I see, I know which seeds to cultivate for the truth to flourish. I see the seeds of my joy are tiny, and I know they need quiet and dark spaces to germinate. I see that nothing grows here in my garden without the light of my attention, without the water of my intention. And so I know, and so I grow, and so I dance with all the aspects of living, happily tending my garden, praising God as I do my work, praising God to have work to do, grateful for the tools of my hands, and my heart, and the Son, and the wind and the rain, grateful for all of it.

I rejoice in bringing the fruits of me to the market place of the present moment. I love to exchange with all the other gardeners. The marketplace of this moment is abundant as we exchange our fruit and nourish each other with what we have observed and learned while tending our gardens. All of this we do under the Son. I celebrate those God directs to my heart to be nourished, and I offer what has been grown in me, knowing it is One in the same.

REVEL AND GIVE THANKS

We revel and give thanks for the broad community of God's creation, and the specific and perfect elements of that community that are present with us, and in us.

We desire to understand the truth, and we acknowledge that all the help we need is here right now.

We let the noise of the world fall away and we bask in the radiance of the Truth that is never gone from us but only at times eclipsed.

We express our willingness to be shown what is real, and our willingness to let go of what we have thought to hold instead. And we are so grateful to hear the voice of truth speak to us.

We trust this practice and we open our minds and our bodies to correction.

We focus on our intention instead of effort, and we accept, trust and love all that we are being shown in each moment.

WE GIVE THANKS

We give thanks for the cool breeze, the warm sun and the delicious way they meet on our skin.

We give thanks for the spacious and warm hearts of our friends and families and the way our hearts find a home in their hearts.

We give thanks for the inspiration we receive in seeing others love what they love, and so we learn to trust what we love.

We give thanks for a growing awareness of Truth and the release from fear that it brings.

We give thanks for the joy that rises up in our hearts on wings of praise for all of this.

It renews us and re-creates us as we notice All that Is right now.

SOLSTICE

The planets turn as the external light shrinks from our view. Every earthly event, every human happening, has its deepest meaning in its capacity to illustrate the truth. The contrast of these dark days creates new awareness, and my experience is subject to my awareness. The dark exposes the light shining within me. It shows me the light of my heart, and helps me find the warmth of its glow. It's a homecoming.

My acknowledgment and gratitude throw the light of my heart up like a spotlight, throw it out like a searchlight. Let every heart be searched, let every heart be spotted. Let every One be re-minded.

When I reach into the flame of Love my hand finds faith to hold. When I extend into the sea of Love, I scatter the light of my faith to every corner. Whatever the eyes of my body tell me, my heart knows the deeper meaning. God is real, Love is true, All is well, right now, and forever.

With my feet on the earth, and my heart in God's hand, I see, and my response is reverence for All that is. The Love of God, the Spirit of life is present in equal and infinite measure everywhere, and in everyone. I offer gratitude for the light that reveals everything, and holds me in perfect relationship with the whole of Living. I trust the path that is being marked for me, and I accept the courage provided to move out of small thinking, and into the vast wilderness of the mystery. I know I will be shown according to my capacity to see.

Waking to each day, I look to Love for my work, and I work for the Love that will show me the way. My talents and abilities are designed by Love, built by Love, and move with Love. Love conducts the movement of everything, and I seek to move in this world without the interference of my doubts. Let me receive the wage of my work and be filled with the joy that is generated by sharing. Let me see all the pieces and people in my life, this day, in new ways, as Love would have me see them. Let the cover of past thought be removed so I may discover the present of presence, the gifts that have been placed in me, and add them to the world's treasure.

My challenges are only the meeting of what I am in truth, pushing against the thin skin of what I think I am. I welcome this stretching, grateful that the truth cannot be denied. I trust the laws of cause and effect, knowing they are moving the world in perfect harmony.

Divine intelligence moves me, and moves in me, constantly designing and directing my thinking, my emotions, and my body at the deepest level. I am reminded that this is true for me, and every one I see. My awareness of this allows me to trust, and through my trust I find the way home.

There is power in my choice. I choose to let Love open and move me. I choose to hear the voice of God only. I choose to accept God's Will as my own. I choose to dance the mystery, knowing God will guide my steps perfectly and poetically. I choose to know the fullest purpose of each moment as it holds the map to the deepest experience of my essential beauty.

I know there is a place in each of us that is so beautiful; the angels would weep to look upon it. I know this is the vision of who we really are. I know that when I can stand in the world without covering this place, I will be home at last and forever. And so it is.

I know that when I practice I engage in the action of uncovering myself by mining for stagnation and releasing it. I locate the stuck places using my discomfort and disease as a map. Through Faith I am able to go where my discomforts are and deliver the breath that has been withheld there. Allowing the breath back into these areas releases the holding and frees me. Through the breath I am restored to peace of mind. Through faith I am aware of the help available to me and so I ask, and so I feel the arms of Love surround me as I move through this process, supported and encouraged. I listen for the voice of the Holy Spirit and use it to tune my heart.

My practice is the ladder I use to climb to my highest sense of Self. I acknowledge it as a vehicle and not my destination. I recognize that there are many means of climbing, many practices, and I have love and respect for whatever means my brothers and sisters use to realize the presence of God, knowing each is called and each will answer in their own way. I recognize that the way the spirit directs my own practice may look different day to day but still I see them all as the same in their intention and purpose. And so I remember the only thing I need to remember, that we are One. I know I do not need to look for Love, as Love is what I am. Remembering this I acknowledge the Love all around me, in every form. Seeing every human expression as an out-picturing of the call to turn away from mere ideas of Love and return to our home in perfect peace.

Two Left Feet

In this idea of right or wrong, I take issue only with the "or." Right and wrong I can swallow. Aspects, inclusive of the All I have no problem with. I identify with the whole of the vitality moving through me, and the actions that manifest accordingly. I acknowledge and respect the dance of it all.

Sometimes I move with the flow effortlessly, a wise and experienced dancer, graceful, aware, and faithfully in tune. And sometimes I am two left feet. I am, and I am all of it, and all of it is necessary as I move to stand under, and understand what is. And so I love, and love myself in every form, every manifestation, in every other I see. I simply walk past my inclination to judge, and condemn. I move with the confidence of one held precious in God's sight. This is what I am even when I am stepping on toes. I will not question my integrity this day as I feel and know more than anything I am complete. It's my deep and steadfast intention to Love directly, immediately, and constantly from the place I find myself in this moment.

Face Of Truth

Peace of mind comes from the acceptance of our unity. Unity excludes nothing. Do not over look the face of Truth gazing back at you through every fault you find in another. Look past the temptation to judge. It will only bring you suffering.

Quiet

Letting the noise of the world slow and grow still even the slightest bit, gives me new perspective and a glimpse into the sounds of silence.

I practice using my attention to locate this vast resource. I relax and give my mind and my body to the breath. It broadly and specifically guides me into alignment with every other, as we move from the singular source of Love. And moving from the same source makes it impossible to be apart from each other. Knowing this, I celebrate every thing I see for the beauty that it is. Moving from the single source of Love, I can let go of effort and be carried to the doorstep of every heart. I go with the flow, and know as I go, that I go with God. I let the breath quiet the busy mind that second guesses, knowing I am held perfectly in the arms of God right now. There is no other real place for me to be. I can only dream of another place and while I sometimes I do, I can also let it go again with the next exhale.

I carry no concerns about missing anything that is calling for my action. I know it will patiently visit me, over and over until finally I hear my cue and play my particular part in God's plan for salvation. I cannot be late in Truth, only in judgment. This is good to know.

The Exercise Of Prayer

This practice is a means. If you are holding it in such a way as to squeeze, your breath, you must loosen your grip. Focus instead on your intention, not the external form that is taking shape. Leave that to faith.
Be expectantly joyful and graciously receive every form born of your faithful intention to embody the vision of perfect Love. Look for exercises in enlightenment, not more training to guard against what scares you. You will recognize the difference. One involves surrender, the other degrees of clutching.

The seeds of truth fly from God's hand. They catch the wind of any and every heart calling for Truth, and move toward them. Infinite seeds are sown answering the infinite calls to God inherent in every breath moving in every body. The seeds fly and so they move toward the heart that calls, toward every heart.

When they arrive, they find varied conditions. Sometimes they arrive and the heart that is calling is closed, and so the seed remains, unopened. Some find an open heart but they are not planted well. There is not enough resolve to dissolve the inhibitions and the seed remains present, but still unopened.

And sometimes they arrive, to find a heart fully open. The soil is rich with faith, and the gardener is awake and attentive, ready and willing to give his mind to the wisdom of the seeds source, with the full conviction that his hands will be perfectly guided to bring the seed to full maturity.

Through faith the seed is soaked and opens. Through faith the sprout is planted and takes root. Through faith the plant pushes through the soil of illusion and rises upward, growing tall in a world hungry for comfort.

Those consciously willing to receive and parent these seeds, become the forest of the faithful. They are visible reminders of God's presence. They are reminders that Love is alive and well in this moment.

When we feel lost we can always look up and see these witnesses for God standing tall, pointing the way home. We only need to let our hearts call, and open the soil of our being to the seeds of Truth.

You don't need the specific form of this practice, but if you allow it to, if you intend it to, this, or any practice, will carry you to what you do need. It will carry you toward a remembrance of who you are, of what you are.

This practice, any practice will serve your most earnest intention. If you fearfully intend to avoid the truth by burying your perfection in shame and guilt, comparing yourself to others, feeling you are less or more, then so your practice shall show you that belief constantly, and in infinite forms.

If your intention is to remember who you are, beautiful and unique, made in God's image and loved completely, you must be willing to forgive and let go of what you are not.

What you believe you need will be the heart of any practice you undertake, and will ultimately determine your life. Remember the perfection of your maker and know you could not be of God and be anything other than beautiful. Use your practice, your life, to listen to the voice deep inside you, the voice under the fears and projections, the voice that tells you what is true.

This practice is a vehicle, a tool to dig through the layers of training and prejudice all the way down to the simple joy of being, the simple joy of living. If you use your practice for the intended purpose of uncovering your truth, it will release you from the small space your fears have persuaded you to accept. Remember that any time you find your self in a dark place, you can simply choose again. You can change your mind. You can quietly step back and look at what you have chosen instead of peace, and let it go because you do not want it.

There is much beauty in the world and beauties are incomparable as each are unto themselves in form, yet they join with each other in essential purpose. Beauty is the intended approach of every soul toward the divine, and each one is worthy. We all approach God in our own way, and each one of us is engaged in the process of peeling away what is not, finding the seed of perfect Love living in our hearts, planting it in our lives, and watching it sprout into the words we speak and the actions we take.

Any practice aimed at anything other than the uncovering of the truth is not of value, it's not alive and it will wither, never bearing any joy. Let your practice live. Let it breathe. Let the spirit move, and move in you, determining the perfect path for you to walk toward the full knowing of your highest good. Be patient and generous with every part of yourself, with every brother and sister, compassionately remembering they are engaged in the very same.

As you practice and make your way home, with little steps, with big steps, remember there is no step, no effort less or more than another, They are all the same in intention. Accept them all, trust them all, love them all.

Set your highest intention to know and… breathe. You will be lovingly carried the rest of the way.

And This Is What It Looks Like

Blessed one, you are welcome, and I welcome you, to continue in your process with my added blessing. Keep an expectant eye out for the sponsors in this world who are waiting to provide support for you to let every part find place and relationship to the whole. I am holding your story, and the larger intention that it is outlining for your whole heart. You are doing it, and this is what it looks like. Do not be led into temptation. Your intention to give everything you are into the loving hands of God will, and is, delivering you from every evil, which is really just one evil. It is one evil that comes in a million colors–the lie that you could be other than precious. Accept the gift of Christ's vision and let it all shake out. Do not doubt when you feel the strain of attempting to hold opposing thought systems. It is not without sensation and it is fool proof. The Holy Spirit will answer your every call for help. I wish you comfort this day as you move, and move through as you do, as you can. My continued love and blessings pour out to you always and forever my friend.

The Same

I am a raging waterfall.
Poetry falls from my heart constantly.
You can swim or drown.
They are the same to me.
I will not stop.

Published by One Body Books
1711 West 116th Street
Indianapolis, Indiana USA 46032

Messages to Me:
Words Collected on the Road to Silence
Copyright © 2007 by Margaret Coyle.

Design:
Susanna Dulkinys and UDN | United Designers Network
San Francisco, California and Berlin, Germany
www.uniteddesigners.com

Photography:
Ray Takuji Sato lives and works in San Francisco.
www. wabishi.com

Printing:
Ruksaldruck
Berlin, Germany

First Edition

Library of Congress
Cataloging-in-Publication
Data Available
ISBN-13: 978-0-9789468-0-7
ISBN-10: 0-9789468-0-4

ONE BODY BOOKS

1 BODY INC